Bloody Rwanda

The Genocide

Thomas Hodge

For all those that were unable

to speak for themselves

Examining the 1994 Rwandan

Decisions

Of the United Nations

In examining the United Nations decisions during the 1994 Rwandan genocide incident, one can clearly see issues concerning conflicting interests among key actors in the United Nations decision-making process. Throughout the process of the United Nations taking in demands and supports and converting those inputs into decisions, one can clearly see that a breakdown did occur somewhere in the process. The Rwandan genocide has often been seen as one of the United Nations greatest failures. In examining, the incident one will truly be able to see where the process falls apart leading to the deaths of hundreds of thousands of people by means of systematic annihilation. One should take into consideration that the United Nations was created following World War II for the purpose of advancing a respect for human rights as can be seen in the first article of the U.N. Charter (United Nations, 1985). In light of the purpose of the United Nations, one can easily determine that the organization had failed to uphold its original purposes due to the great amount of lives that had been lost in Rwanda.

In examining the demands that were placed on the international political system, several key actors should be addressed that were relevant in the situation. Firstly, the Tutsi population of Rwanda was a population that ideally should have been requesting relief from their persecution. Contrarily, many Tutsi refugees were not fully aware of the extent to which the killings had occurred reach until several weeks into the incident (Kuperman, 2000). The voice of the Tutsi people of Rwanda were heavily silenced until after several decisions had been laid out by the UN. This could be seen as being affected by their lack of governmental representation due to the assassination of the Rwandan

President. The peacekeepers of the U.N. Assistance Mission for Rwanda (UNAMIR) had a great demand for further assistance in Rwanda as the commander of the mission had sent communications to the Secretariat attempting to notify the Security Council of possible violence prior to the Rwandan President's assassination.

Many of the non-governmental organizations such as the Red Cross, African Rights, and the Human Rights Watch demanded international intervention to avoid catastrophic loss of lives. It was clear that such organizations were appalled by acts of clear genocide. These organizations demanded that a peacekeeping force step in to stop the violence that was occurring in the country and prevent the slaughter of hundreds of thousands of people. The non-governmental organizations also demand protection for their own people that were in Rwanda.

The states that would be assisting Rwanda if a decision was made to intervene had demands of non-involvement. The western countries had a demand upon the system to reduce their losses. This can clearly be seen as Belgium withdrew its peacekeeping forces from Rwanda after sustaining causalities during the first few days of the reaction to the Rwandan President's assassination. Many larger actors in the organization like the United States, France, and the United Kingdom demanded that more information be given as to the legitimacy of allegations of genocide.

They did not wish to overstep the boundaries of infringing on states sovereignty and did not wish commit personnel or funds if only warranted by a typical civil war in an African nation. Neighboring countries of Rwanda had concerns regarding an influx of refugees pouring across their borders. Some of these countries include Uganda, Zaire, and Tanzania. These neighboring countries could see an overwhelming number of refugees as an unwanted burden (Kuperman, 2000).

The countries of France and Belgium had provided a degree of support to the United Nations effort by providing a peacekeeping force to aid in maintaining the peace in Rwanda prior to the outbreak of genocide. These countries along with the United States also had provided the United Nations with a great deal of financial support through dues and funding. This could be seen that they were vested in the organization to either improve their own interest or that they intended on promoting the values established in the UN charter. The

countries of Uganda and Tanzania did

pay dues to the United Nations and

maintain membership but to a much

lesser degree than the larger

countries. The NGOs like the Human

Rights Watch and Red Cross had

provided the organization with

valuable information and expert

advice about the situation unfolding

in Rwanda.

The decision-making process of the

United Nations was carried out

through a series of discussions and

reviews. The overlapping norm that comes into light with the Rwandan genocide is one of the guiding principles of the UN that were laid out in the first article of the UN charter which is to promote the respect for human rights. To protect human rights seems to be fairly straight-forward until it comes into conflict with infringing on a state's sovereignty. This clash of values led to an ethical dilemma in the UN as to how to approach the issue with Rwanda. The delays allowed the perpetrators of the genocide ample time to carry out the killing of hundreds of thousands of people. The rules and procedures to make a determination as to what was going on in Rwanda were effectively used against the organization to decrease its effectiveness in resolving the issue.

The Hutu majority in Rwanda that was carrying out the systematic killing was aware that the United Nations would not step in unless they had clear evidence of genocide. Knowing this, they made efforts to avoid mass killings in the view of foreigners (Kuperman, 2000). The well-hidden genocide resulted in debates among the permanent members of the UN Security Council and the non-permanent members of the council. The United Nations debated on the appropriate actions to take in Rwanda over several months. The debate began well before the genocide started. On the day prior to the Rwandan President's assassination, the UN Security Council had recalled several support elements of the UNIMAR in *Resolution 909* (United Nations Security Council, 1994a). This initial decision was made even though the council was concerned over violence and issues with degradation in security, humanitarian and health situation of Rwanda. In making the decisions, the United States and France did have a great influence in the decisions of the United Nations as they were permanent members of the Security Council with substantial contributions to the organization in the form of UN financial dues and personnel support. The Human Rights Watch also did have some influence on the organization as it provided information to the organization and advice from subject matter experts.

There were several possible alternative avenues of approach to the situation in Rwanda. Kuperman (2000) outlined the possibilities of direct U.S. military mobilization in an effort to halt the genocide. Several possible levels of intervention were examined. A major issue with U.S. military intervention would have been the time in which it would have taken to deploy troops to Rwanda rapid enough to be effective in curtailing the genocide. Kuperman found that rapid deployment of troops would have saved between 50,000 and 100,000 lives depending on the level of response. This would have involved a great deal of U.S. investment into the Rwandan incident. This would not have been highly beneficial to the United States as Rwanda was seen as a strategically unimportant country.

Through several Security Council

resolutions, one can see that the genocide in Rwanda had gradually become clear. The descriptions of the violence Rwanda evolved through the resolutions and reports to become more vivid. *Resolution 912* of the Security Council referred to the violence in Rwanda as "mindless violence and carnage which are engulfing Rwanda" (United Nations Security Council, 1994b). The reports were still hesitant of referring to the situation as genocide even weeks into the incident. In June, *Resolution*

925 endorsed the augmentation of UNAMIR in Rwanda with two additional battalions of support (United Nations Security Council, 1994c). A month later, *Resolution 935* established a commission of experts to investigate the allegations of genocide and provide reports that would identify the individuals responsible for the violations of humanitarian laws (United Nations Security Council, 1994d). Finally, the Security Council of the United Nations established the International Tribunal for Rwanda in *Resolution 955* to prosecute the individuals in Rwanda that were responsible for the genocide (United Nations Security Council, 1994e). These decisions were reached based on pressures placed on the hegemonic states of the U.N. to abide by the mission of the UN charter in upholding the basic human rights of Rwandan people.

United Nations produced several decisions in relation to the demands placed on it due to the genocide in Rwanda. The United Nations' final decision on the matter involved the creation of the International Tribunal for Rwanda. This tribunal had the task of making determinations on the guilt or innocence of individuals that took part or instigated the mass killings of Tutsis and Hutu sympathizers. Leading up to that final decision to try individuals involved in the genocide, the United Nations also set forth a group of experts to make determinations of which individuals to pursue based on evidence provided through investigations conducted by various groups. These final decisions of the Security Council of the United Nations reflected the morals and values set forth in the original UN Charter that founded the organization. This decision also provided the Tutsi of Rwanda with some justice for the crimes committed against more than half a million Rwandan Tutsis.

In *Resolution 955,* the United Nations Security council set forth a precedent in clearly defining genocide to include the act of rape which had not been listed formerly listed in descriptions of what genocide was (United Nations Security Council, 1994e). The annex provided in the resolution gave grounds to a better understanding of crimes against humanity. Prior to *Resolution 955,* the Geneva Conventions stood as the document that was most descriptive of human rights laws, but due to the wording of the Geneva Conventions, much room was left for interpretation. In the decision laid out by the UN, human rights were clearly defined with a greater degree of certainty. The defining of genocide in the document allows for international organizations to more clearly recognize genocide at an earlier point in time for the purpose of preventing greater loss of life and reducing the number of human rights violations if there was to be a similar incident.

The reaction from the UN represents both a functional system and dysfunctional system. The effectiveness of the UN response can easily be questioned due in part to the fact there were few Tutsis that had not been eradicated in Rwanda when a decision was reached. Research shows that the killings lessened when the UN responded to the crisis, but also it shows that the Hutu majority had also began to run out of Tutsis to eradicate in the country (Kuperman, 2000). The fact that response was too late for more than half a million Tutsis who had been systematically killed displays a dysfunctional system. For system to be effective, it must respond to the problem in a timely manner. An example of this principle would be a scientist attempting to prolong the lives of individuals born in the 1920s to allow them to live past the age of eighty. If the scientist only develops a solution in 2010, this does not help the part of the population that would have died before the age of eighty from the sample group. Likewise, the Tutsi who had been the targets of the genocide killings were not alive to receive the solution provided by the UN when it was presented in the summer of 1994. The hegemonic powers of the UN, such as the US, managed to receive adequate response to its demands of minimizing US costs associated with the Rwandan incident. The main US causality in the Rwandan incident would be the image of the United States due to its lack of effective response to the incident.

As a functional system, the UN did manage to respond to the demands placed on it throughout the decision-making process concerning the clarity of defining humanitarian rights in general and genocide in particular. This was accomplished as a result of *Resolution 955*. The fact that a determination was made did follow the flow of a functional system when disregarding the timeliness of the response. The UN did make changes to the environment produce feedback to the cycle of the political system as a result of the incident. This would show that it was functional in the most basic definitions of the systems theory.

In conclusion, the Rwanda genocide of 1994 served to show several weakness and strengths in the United Nations decision-making process. As a weakness, one can easily stress timeliness and fear of taking action as a weakness. In all five UN Security Council resolutions, the last statement is the same. "[The Security Council] decides to remain actively seized of the question."(United Nations Security Council, 1994a, b, c, d, & e).   This statement is polite way saying that the Security Council would simply wait to see what unfolds. The waiting to see what would happen was the weakness in the process that reduced the effectiveness of the UN in promoting human rights. As strength, the process could be seen as effectively not crossing the sovereignty of states through the process. The process also allowed for the hegemonic states of the process to weld their power in way to keep them from becoming too deeply associated with the incident directly. The Rwanda genocide truly serves an example of the UN being very good at adjusting policies on paper to define concepts, such as genocide, on paper once an issue is brought forth but being slow to react to such acts in a timely manner.

References

Kuperman, A. J. (2000). Rwanda in Retrospect. *Foreign Affairs*, *79*(1), 94-118.

United Nations. (1985). *Charter of the United Nations and Statute of the International Court of Justice.* New York, NY. Department of Public Information.

United Nations Security Council. (1994) *Resolution 909.*New York, NY. Department of Public Information.

United Nations Security Council. (1994) *Resolution 912.*New York, NY. Department of Public Information.

United Nations Security Council. (1994) *Resolution 925.*New York, NY. Department of Public Information.

United Nations Security Council. (1994) *Resolution 935.*New York, NY. Department of Public

Information.

United Nations Security Council. (1994) *Resolution 955.*New York, NY. Department of Public Information.